THE BOOK OF THE LOVER AND THE BELOVED

D1384092

THE BOOK
OF THE LOVER AND
THE BELOVED

Edited by
KENNETH LEECH
from the E. Allison Peers translation
of Ramon Lull

PAULIST PRESS
New York, N.Y./Ramsey, N.J./Toronto

First Published in Great Britain by
SPCK in 1946
Reprinted in a revised edition by ·
Sheldon Press in 1978

Copyright © SPCK

ISBN: 0-8091-2135-2

Library of Congress
Catalog Card number: 78-61666

Published in the United States by
Paulist Press
Editorial office: 1865 Broadway, N.Y., N.Y. 10023
Business office: 545 Island Road, Ramsey, N.J. 07446

Printed and bound in the
United States of America

TABLE OF CONTENTS

PREFACE

The Book of the Lover and the Beloved was translated from Catalan by the late Professor Allison Peers in 1923, and subsequently revised in 1946 for the SPCK edition. The text printed here is substantially that of Peers, but I have taken the liberty of slightly modernizing the language, and at certain points simplifying the punctuation. This is not therefore a new translation, but an attempt to present Peers' text in a form which may appeal to a wider audience.

KENNETH LEECH

INTRODUCTION

RAMON LULL (1232–1316) was a native of Palma in Majorca, then part of a kingdom which had for a long period been in Muslim possession, and had only recently been reconquered by King James I of Catalonia-Aragon in 1229. Large numbers of Moors were still living there, as were many Jews, and the young Ramon was brought into contact at an early age with a variety of religious traditions and ethnic groups. This early experience was of decisive significance for the development of his thought and his theological concerns.

His early life was that of a page at the royal court, and during this period he composed many love lyrics after the pattern of the troubadours, which he sang to his mistresses. His marriage to Blanca Picany, some time before 1257, seems to have made little difference to his pattern of life. However, at the age of thirty, while composing a troubadour song, he received a vision of Christ crucified, which was repeated five times. From this moment, he says, his sole desire was to serve God and to preach the Gospel. So he became a 'Fool of Love', a holy troubadour singing of the Love of God.

Soon after this, he heard a sermon on St Francis Day, and he was strongly drawn to the Franciscan

1

ideal of poverty and self-giving love. As a result he later became a Tertiary, a member of the Franciscan Third Order, indeed 'the most distinguished tertiary of the thirteenth or indeed of any other century.'[1] Earlier, however, it was the Dominican influence of Ramon de Penyafort, the former Master-General of the Dominican Order, which had encouraged him to study at Majorca in order to acquire some basic knowledge of Arabic. For, soon after his accession in 1276, King James II had set up, at Ramon's inspiration, a missionary college at Miram in Majorca to train missionaries in Arabic and in the understanding of Islam. Here Ramon studied and taught, and in 1285 he persuaded Pope Honorius III to set up a school of Arabic in Rome. Ramon's future life was to be very largely dominated by the Arabic-speaking world of Islam, and his strong desire to preach the Gospel there and to seek a synthesis of Christian and Muslim theological thought.

In 1291 Acre fell, and Syria was evacuated. It meant the end of Christian work in vast areas of the east. The following year, at the age of sixty, Ramon Lull set out for North Africa. He landed at Tunis but, after a short attempt at preaching, he was arrested and deported. Fifteen years later, in 1307, he was back in North Africa. In the streets of Bugia he is alleged to have cried out, 'The law of the Christians is holy and true, and the sect of the Moors is false and wrong, and this I am prepared to prove.' So he was taken into custody, but he carried on his evangelistic activity in prison, and was later deported again.

In 1314, at the age of eighty-two, he again set out for Bugia, where he stayed for a little while, before moving to Tunis. There he was received by the Moors, and he debated in the villages. But at the end of 1315 he returned to Bugia where he was battered to death.

Lull was beatified by Pope Pius IX and a special Mass and Office was allowed in Majorca and throughout the Franciscan Order. His literary output was vast, amounting to nearly five hundred published works, and many others have been ascribed to him. Among his most important writings are *The Book of the Gentile and the Three Wise Men*, an allegory of a travelling Gentile who meets a Jew, a Christian, and a Saracen; *The Book of Contemplation*, a seven-volume work originally written in Arabic; *The Hundred Names of God*, and *The Book of the Tartar and the Christian* (on the Athanasian Creed), both written in Rome; *Felix or The Book of Marvels*, written in Paris; *The Book of the Five Wise Men*; *The Tree of Science*; and the present work.

Although a whole tradition of Lullism grew up after his death, Lull was in general not an original theological thinker, but a rather conventional Augustinian who held that the inquiring mind could acquire all truth. His teaching on the 'Great Art' was held to place too much emphasis on the place of reason, and it was doubts about his orthodoxy in this area which prevented his canonization in 1376. Throughout his writing there is very strong emphasis on reason. Memory and will, he tells us, join and ascend the mountain of the Beloved, so that reason too should rise. Lull seemed to have little or no place for darkness or the *via negativa* in his scheme except as a temporary phenomenon. His concern to refute the heresy of Averroism, with its doctrine of the total separation of God from the world and of the eternity of matter, led him to the opposite position of virtually identifying theological with philosophical truth. Hillgarth notes that 'the somewhat old-fashioned' nature of Lull's philosophy which belongs in many ways more to the twelfth century than to his own age must in large part be ascribed simply to his lack of contact, during his years of study, with any leading centre of Christian thought.'[2] Yet there is also in Lull a Franciscan tenderness and a devotion to the Passion and to the love of God. He was deeply influenced by St Bonaventure, not only in his view that the creation of the world by God could be demonstrated by the light of reason, but also in his belief that all human wisdom, when compared with mystical illumination, was folly. Nevertheless, his view of illumination was intellectual. God, he held, consisted of a series of essential attributes. But the instruments of God's creative work in the world are the Dignities, absolute transcendental principles. In *The Art of Contemplation*, they are said to be nine in number: Goodness, Greatness, Eternity, Power, Wisdom, Will, Virtue, Truth, and Glory. Through these principles, closely similar to Plato's Ideas, all created perfection is brought about. Every element in creation is a symbol of the presence of God.

Lull's vision of the world was essentially that of Neo-Platonism. There was a hierarchy of creation, stretching from God, through the spiritual world and the celestial spheres, to the spheres of the four elements, to man, the animals, and matter. The Divine Dignities exercised their power throughout the created order. Although the actual word 'Dignities' seems to be peculiar to Lull, the idea of 'Divine Attributes' is extremely ancient, appearing in the Old Testament Wisdom literature, in Plotinus, Pseudo-Dionysius, and Augustine among others. The immediate source of Lull's use of it may have been John Scotus Erigena, the ninth-century Irish thinker. But a similar view of Divine Attributes was held by Muslims and Jews. Lull was acquainted with the works of al-Ghazzali, and this may be the reason for his selection of the Divine Dignities as the basis of his system.

For at the heart of Lull's thought and work is the concern for some kind of synthesis between Arabic and Christian thought, and this emerges in particular in *The Art of Contemplation*. Islam was seen as the greatest obstacle to the conversion of the world. Yet few Christians seemed able or willing to devote their energies to a serious Christian-Islamic dialogue. Apart from Roger Bacon, only Lull did so. Lull's central thesis was that the approach to Islam should be one of conversion by peaceful means, through gentle per-suasion and dialogue. Yet linked with this was a militant ideology of combat and confrontation, and his later years (1287-1316) saw him involved in a continuous battle with Islam. But Lull went further than this. Through intellect and love, he believed that a synthesis between Christian theology and Islam was possible.

In his view, the Holy Trinity was mirrored in the created order. There was a Trinitarian structure of creation, God is seen throughout the created order, and his attributes are active through all the levels of created life. Lull's emphasis on intellectual and even mathematical reasoning makes him closely akin to al-Ghazzali who used geometrical ideas in his scientific theology. Also, deeply rooted in medieval Islam was the *kalām*, or Islamic scholastic theology, which set out a rational apologetic for dogma, based on proof and demonstration. Lull, in disputing with Muslims, sought to prove the truth of Christian dogma by the same necessary reasons (*rationes necessariae*). He insisted that the Trinity and the Incarnation were *more* appropriate to Islamic belief in the Unity and Power of God than Islamic theology itself was. So Lull saw Islam as incomplete rather than false. It is difficult to over-stress the degree to which this view represented an advance on the conventional thinking of his age. However, Lull did not believe that reason could replace grace in the work of conversion, and at the end of *The Book of the Gentile*, the Gentile traveller, having listened to the expositions of Jew, Christian, and Muslim, is still left undecided.

Lull's recognition of the essential place of Divine grace 'brought with it a tolerance and objectivity rare for the age, and an emphasis on the necessity for free, not forced, conversion.'[3]

6

And, in spite of his exaltation of reason, Lull is remembered most of all as the 'Fool of Love'. The approach to Christ through folly is deeply embedded in the Franciscan tradition: it is here that we find 'the most developed form of western folly for Christ's sake'.[4] St Francis himself had claimed that 'the Lord told me that he wanted me to be a new fool in the world; and he did not want to lead us by any other way than by that learning'.[5] So Lull, like Francis before him, saw himself as one of God's *joglars* who, unlike the earthly *joglars*, sang only of the love of God.

> I desire to be a fool
> that I may give honour and glory
> to God, and
> I will have no art nor device in my words
> by reason of the greatness of my love.

And so in the book *Blanquerna*, sometimes wrongly described as an autobiography, Lull appears before the Papal Court as a Fool. As a troubadour is intoxicated with the love of his lady, so Lull is intoxicated with the love of Christ his Beloved.

The present work, *The Book of the Lover and the Beloved*, is a small part of the larger work *Blanquerna*, which may date from Lull's time at Miramar. It is a somewhat extravagant religious romance. A wealthy youth, Evast, marries the beautiful Aloma, and after years without a child, a boy, Blanquerna, is born to them. In due course, he leaves them to pursue the solitary life. He wanders into a wood, but later is chosen as the abbot of a monastery, then as bishop,

7

and finally as Pope. But he ends his time as a hermit in the mountains. *The Book of the Lover and the Beloved* may have been written before *Blanquerna*, and was subsequently incorporated into it as Chapter 99. It was composed as a guide to contemplation, with a short passage for every day of the year. The language is that of human love, and it belongs to the long tradition of mystical writing in which the relationship of God and the soul is portrayed in the terms of sexual love. In his description of the origin of the work, Lull also explains its purpose.

> Blanquerna was in prayer and considered the manner wherein to contemplate God and his virtues; and when he had ended his prayer he wrote down the manner in which he had contemplated God. And he did this daily, and brought new arguments to his prayer, so that after many and varied manners he should compose *The Book of the Lover and the Beloved*, and that these manners should be brief, and that in a short space of time, the soul should learn to reflect in many ways. And with the blessing of God, Blanquerna began the book which he divided into as many verses as there are days in the year, and each verse suffices for the contemplation of God in one day, according to the art of the *Book of Contemplation*.

May the reading of this book lead its users to a deeper love of God the Beloved, and to a deep inner transformation of themselves in love.

REFERENCES

1 J. R. H. Moorman, *A History of the Franciscan Order.* (1968), 225.

2 J. N. Hillgarth, *Ramon Lull and Lullism in Fourteenth Century France.* (1971), 6.

3 Ibid., 24.

4 John Saward, 'The Fool for Christ's Sake in Monasticism East and West', in A. M. Allchin (ed.), *Theology and Prayer.* (1975), 37.

5 *Speculum Perfectionis*, 68.

THE WAY IN WHICH
THE HERMIT BLANQUERNA
MADE
THE BOOK OF THE LOVER
AND THE BELOVED

ONE DAY the hermit who was in Rome . . . went to visit the other hermits and recluses who were in Rome, and found that in certain matters they had many temptations, because they did not know how to live in the way which was most suitable for their state. So he thought that he would go to Blanquerna the hermit, and urge him to make a book which would deal with the life of the hermit, and that through this book he would learn and be able to maintain the other hermits in contemplation and devotion. When Blanquerna was at prayer one day, that hermit came to his cell and urged him to write the above-mentioned book. Blanquerna thought for a long time about the way in which he would make the book and what should be in it.

While Blanquerna was thinking in this way, he decided that he would give himself fervently to adoring and contemplating God, so that in prayer God would show him the way in which he should make the book and also what should be in it. While

Blanquerna wept and adored, and God made his soul rise to the furthest limit of its strength in contemplation of him, Blanquerna felt himself carried away in spirit through the great fervour and devotion which he had. And he thought to himself: the strength of love knows no bounds when the Lover loves the Beloved with a very fervent love. As a result, it came to Blanquerna that he should make a Book of the Lover and the Beloved in which the Lover should be a faithful and devout Christian, and the Beloved should be God.

While Blanquerna was thinking along these lines, he remembered that once when he was the Pope, a Saracen had told him that they had certain religious men, including some men called Sufis who are very highly respected by them. These men have words of love and short examples which communicate great devotion to men. They are words which need exposition, and through the exposition of them the understanding soars up high, and so does the will, with an increase of devotion. When Blanquerna had thought about this, he decided to make the book in the way mentioned above, and he ordered the hermit to return to Rome, telling him that soon he would send, with the deacon, *The Book of the Lover and the Beloved*. Through this, for ever, fervour and devotion would be increased among hermits, for it would seek to inspire them with the love of God.

PROLOGUE

Blanquerna was in prayer, considering the way in which to contemplate God and his virtues. When he had ended his prayer, he wrote down the way in which he had contemplated God, and he did this every day, bringing new ideas to his prayer, so that, with many different approaches, he should compose *The Book of the Lover and the Beloved*, and that these approaches should be brief, so that in a short time the soul might learn to reflect in many ways. Blanquerna began the book with God's blessing. He divided it into as many verses as there are days in the year. Each verse is sufficient for the contemplation of God in one day, according to the art of the *Book of Contemplation*.

THE BOOK OF THE LOVER
AND THE BELOVED

★1★

THE Lover asked his Beloved if there was anything remaining in him which was still to be loved. And the Beloved answered that he still had to love that by which his own love could be increased.

★2★

The paths by which the Lover seeks his Beloved are long and perilous. They are populated by considerations, sighs, and tears. They are lit up by love.

★3★

Many lovers come together to love One alone, their Beloved, who made them all to abound in love. And each one had the Beloved as his precious possession, and his thoughts of him were very pleasant, making him suffer a pain which brought delight.

★4★

The Lover wept and said, 'How long will it be until the darkness of the world is past, when the paths to hell will be no more? When will the hour come in which water, which flows downwards, will change its nature and mount upwards? When will the innocent be more in number than the guilty?'

* 5 *

'Ah! When will the Lover joyfully lay down his life for the Beloved? And when will the Beloved see the Lover grow faint for love of him?'

* 6 *

The Lover said to the Beloved, 'You who fill the sun with splendour, fill my heart with love.' The Beloved answered, 'If you did not possess fullness of love, your eyes would not have shed those tears, nor would you have come to this place to see him who loves you.'

* 7 *

The Beloved tested his Lover to see if his love for him were perfect. He asked him how the Beloved's presence differed from his absence. The Lover answered, 'As knowledge and remembrance differ from ignorance and oblivion.'

* 8 *

The Beloved asked the Lover, 'Have you remembered any way in which I have rewarded you for you to love me thus?' 'Yes,' replied the Lover, 'for I make no distinction between the trials which you send and the joys.'

★ 9 ★

The Beloved asked, 'Tell me, Lover, if I double your sorrows, will you still be patient?' 'Yes,' replied the Lover, 'so that you will also double my love.'

★ 10 ★

The Beloved said to the Lover, 'Do you know yet what love means?' The Lover answered, 'If I did not know the meaning of love, I would know the meaning of trial, sorrow, and pain.'

★ 11 ★

They asked the Lover, 'Why do you not answer the Beloved when he calls you?' He replied, 'I brave great dangers so that I can come to him, and I speak to him, desiring his honours.'

★ 12 ★

'Foolish Lover! Why do you weary your body, cast away your wealth, and leave the joys of this world, going around like an outcast among the people?' He replied, 'To honour the honours of my Beloved, for he is neglected and dishonoured by more men than those who honour and love him.'

15

'Tell us, Fool of Love! Which can be seen better, the Beloved in the Lover, or the Lover in the Beloved?' The Lover answered and said, 'By love the Beloved can be seen. By sighs and tears, by trials and pain the Lover can be seen.'

The Lover sought for one who would tell his Beloved what great trials he was enduring for love of him, and how he was near to dying. And he found his Beloved who was reading a book in which were written all the griefs which love made him suffer for his Beloved, and the joys which he had from his love.

Our Lady presented her Son to the Lover so that he might kiss his feet and so that in his book he might write about the virtues of Our Lady.

'Tell us, singing bird! Have you placed yourself in the care of my Beloved so that he may guard you from indifference and increase your love in you?' The bird replied, 'And who makes me sing but the Lord of love who regards indifference as sin?'

★ 17 ★

Between fear and hope, Love has made her home. She lives on thought, and dies of forgetfulness, the foundations of which are the delights of this world.

★ 18 ★

There was a conflict between the eyes and the memory of the Lover. The eyes said that it was better to behold the Beloved than to remember him. But Memory said that remembrance brings tears to the eyes and makes the heart burn with love.

★ 19 ★

The Lover inquired from Understanding and Will which of them was the nearer to his Beloved. The two ran, and Understanding came nearer to the Beloved than did Will.

★ 20 ★

There was strife between the Lover and the Beloved. Another lover saw it and wept until peace and concord were made between the Beloved and the Lover.

★ 21 ★

Sighs and Tears came to be judged by the Beloved, and they asked him which of them loved him the more deeply. The Beloved's judgement was that sighs were nearer to love, and tears to the eyes.

★ 22 ★

The Lover came to drink from the fountain which gives love to him who has none, and his griefs redoubled. The Beloved came to drink from that fountain so that the love of one whose griefs were doubled might be doubled too.

★ 23 ★

The Lover was sick and thought about the Beloved who fed him from his merits, quenched his thirst with love, made him rest in patience, clothed him with humility, and gave him truth for medicine.

★ 24 ★

They asked the Lover where his Beloved was. 'See him for yourselves,' he answered, 'in a house nobler than all the nobility of creation. But see him too in my love, my griefs and my tears.'

★ 25 ★

They said to the Lover, 'Where are you going?' He answered, 'I come from my Beloved.' 'Where do you come from?' 'I go to my Beloved.' 'When will you return?' 'I shall be with my Beloved.' 'How long will you be with your Beloved?' 'For as long as my thoughts remain on him.'

★ 26 ★

The birds sang dawn hymns, and the Lover who is the Dawn, woke. The birds ended their song, and the Lover died in the dawn for his Beloved.

★ 27 ★

The bird sang in the garden of the Beloved. The Lover came and said to the bird, 'If we do not understand one another in speech, we can make ourselves understood by love, for in your song I see my Beloved before my eyes.'

★ 28 ★

The Lover wanted to sleep for he had worked hard seeking his Beloved, and he was afraid that he might forget him. And he wept for fear that he might fall asleep and might not remember his Beloved.

★ 29 ★

The Lover and the Beloved met, and the Beloved said to the Lover, 'You do not need to speak to me. Simply sign to me with your eyes—for they are words to my heart—that I may give you what you ask from me.'

19

The Lover was disobedient to his Beloved, and the Lover wept. And the Beloved came in the vesture of his Lover and died, so that his Lover might regain what he had lost. So he gave him a gift which was greater than that which he had lost.

The Beloved filled his Lover with love, and did not grieve for his tribulations for they would simply make him love more deeply. In the greatest of his tribulations the Lover found delight and refreshment.

The Lover said, 'The secrets of my Beloved torture me, for my deeds reveal them, and my mouth keeps them secret and does not reveal them to anyone.'

This is Love's contract: the Lover must be long-suffering, patient, humble, fearful, diligent, and trustful; he must be ready to face great dangers for the honour of his Beloved. And his Beloved is pledged to be true and free, merciful and just, with his Lover.

★ 34 ★

The Lover set out over hill and plain in search of devotion, to see if his Beloved was well served. But in every place he found that devotion was very inadequate. So he delved into the earth to see if he could find more perfect devotion there than there was above ground.

★ 35 ★

'O bird, you sing of love. Ask my Beloved who has taken me to be his servant why he tortures me with love.' The bird replied, 'If love did not make you bear trials, how could you show your love for him?'

★ 36 ★

The Lover thoughtfully trod the paths of his Beloved. Now he stumbled and fell among the thorns, but they were flowers and a bed of love to him.

★ 37 ★

They asked the Lover, 'Would you change your Beloved for another?' He answered and said, 'Why, what other is better or nobler than the sovereign and eternal Good? For he is infinite in greatness, power, wisdom, love, and perfection.'

The Lover wept and sang songs of his Beloved, saying, 'Swifter is love in the heart of the lover than is the splendour of the lightning to the eye, or the thunder to the ear. The tears of love gather more quickly than the waves of the sea, and sighing is more appropriate to love than whiteness is to snow.'

They asked the Lover, 'In what does your Beloved's glory consist?' He answered, 'He is Glory itself.' They asked him, 'In what does his power consist?' He answered, 'He is Power itself.' 'And in what does his Wisdom consist?' 'He is Wisdom itself.' 'And why is he to be loved?' 'Because he is Love itself.'

The Lover rose early and went to seek his Beloved. He found travellers on the road and asked them if they had seen his Beloved. They answered him, 'When did the eyes of your mind lose sight of your Beloved?' The Lover answered and said, 'Even when my Beloved is no longer in my thoughts, he is never absent from the eyes of my body, for everything that I see shows me my Beloved.'

With eyes of thought and grief, sighs and tears, the Lover gazed upon his Beloved; and with eyes of grace, justice, pity, mercy, and bounty, the Beloved gazed upon his Lover. And the bird sang of that Countenance of which we have spoken already and which was so full of delight.

* 42 *

The keys of the doors of love are gilded with meditations, sighs, and tears. The cord which binds them is woven from conscience, contrition, devotion, and satisfaction. The door is kept by justice and mercy.

* 43 *

The Lover beat on the door of his Beloved with blows of love and hope. The Beloved heard the blows of his Lover with humility, pity, charity, and patience. Deity and Humanity opened the doors, and the Lover went in to his Beloved.

* 44 *

Propriety and Community met, and joined together, so that there might be love and benevolence between Lover and Beloved.

* 45 *

There are two fires which nourish the love of the Lover. One is made of pleasures, desires, and thoughts. The other is composed of fear and grief, weeping and tears.

23

The Lover longed for solitude and he went away to live alone so that he might have the companionship of his Beloved, for he was lonely amongst many people.

The Lover was all alone in the shade of a fair tree. Men passed by that place and they asked him why he was alone. And the Lover answered, 'I am alone now that I have seen you and heard you. Until now I was in the company of my Beloved.'

By signs of love, the Lover held conversation with the Beloved. By means of fear, weeping, tears, and thoughts, the Lover told his griefs to the Beloved.

The Lover was afraid that his Beloved might fail him in his greatest need, and the Beloved took love from his Lover. Then the Lover was sorry and repented in his heart, and the Beloved restored hope and charity to the heart of the Lover, and weeping and tears to his eyes, so that love might return to him.

Whether Lover and Beloved are near or far is all the same, for their love mingles as water mingles with wine. They are joined as heat is with light. They agree and are as closely united as Essence and Being.

* 51 *

The Lover said to his Beloved, 'My healing and my grief are both in you. The more surely you heal me, the greater my grief grows: and the more I languish, the more you give me health.' The Beloved answered, 'Your love is a seal and an imprint by which you show forth my honour before men.'

* 52 *

The Lover saw himself taken and bound, wounded and killed, for the love of his Beloved. Those who tortured him asked him, 'Where is your Beloved?' He answered, 'See him here in the increase of my love, and in the strength which it gives me to bear my torments.'

* 53 *

The Lover said to the Beloved, 'I have never fled from you, nor ceased to love you, since I knew you, for I was always in you, by you, and with you wherever I went.' The Beloved answered, 'Nor, since you have known me and loved me, have I once forgotten you. Never once have I deceived or failed you.'

* 54 *

The Lover went through the city like one who was a fool, singing of his Beloved, and men asked him if he had gone mad. He answered, 'My Beloved has taken my will, and I have yielded up to him my understanding. So there is nothing left in me except memory by which I remember my Beloved.'

* 55 *

The Beloved said, 'It would be a miracle against love if the Lover were to fall asleep and forget his Beloved.' The Lover answered, 'In the same way, it would be a miracle against love if the Beloved did not wake him, since he has desired him.'

* 56 *

The heart of the Lover soared to the heights of the Beloved, so that he might not be prevented from loving him in the abyss of this world. And when he reached his Beloved he contemplated him with sweetness and delight. But the Beloved led him down again to this world so that he might contemplate him in tribulations and griefs.

* 57 *

They asked the Lover, 'In what does all your wealth consist?' He answered, 'In the poverty which I bear for my Beloved.' 'And where is your rest?' 'In the griefs caused me by love.' 'Who is your doctor?' 'The trust that I have in my Beloved.' 'And who is your master?' 'The signs of my Beloved which I see in all creatures.'

★ 58 ★

The bird sang on a branch in leaf and flower, and the breeze stirred the leaves, bearing away the scent of the flowers. 'What does this trembling of leaves and fragrance of flowers mean?' asked the Lover of the bird. The bird answered, 'The trembling of the leaves signifies obedience, and the fragrance of the flowers signifies suffering and adversity.'

★ 59 ★

The Lover went in desire of his Beloved, and he met two friends who greeted and embraced and kissed each other with love and tears. And the Lover swooned, so strongly did these two lovers call his Beloved to mind.

★ 60 ★

The Lover thought of death, and was afraid until he remembered his Beloved. Then he cried in a loud voice to those near him, 'Ah, my friends, have love, so that you will not fear death or danger, in doing honour to my Beloved.'

★ 61 ★

They asked the Lover where his love first began. He answered, 'It began in the glories of my Beloved, and from that beginning I was led to love my neighbour as myself, and to cease to love deception and falsehood.'

* 62 *

'Tell us, Fool of Love! If your Beloved no longer cared for you, what would you do?' 'I should love him still,' he replied, 'or else I must die, because to cease to love is death, and love is life.'

* 63 *

They asked the Lover what he meant by perseverance. 'It is both happiness and sorrow,' he answered, 'in the Lover who always loves, honours, and serves his Beloved with fortitude, patience, and hope.'

* 64 *

The Lover wanted his Beloved to recompense him for the time that he had served him. And the Beloved calculated the thoughts, tears, longings, perils, and trials which his Lover had borne for love of him. The Beloved added to the account eternal bliss, and he gave himself for a recompense to his Lover.

* 65 *

They asked the Lover what he meant by happiness. 'It is sorrow', he replied, 'which is borne for Love.'

28

'Tell us, Fool! What do you mean by sorrow?' 'It is the remembrance of the dishonour done to my Beloved who is worthy of all honour.'

The Lover was gazing on a place where he had seen his Beloved. And he said, 'Ah, place, which recalls the blessed haunts of my Beloved. You will tell my Beloved that I suffer trials and adversities for his sake.' And that place answered, 'When your Beloved hung on me, he bore greater trials and adversities for love of you than all other trials and adversities that Love could give to its servants.'

The Lover said to his Beloved, 'You are all, and through all, and in all, and with all. I will have you wholly that I may have, and be, myself wholly.' The Beloved answered, 'You cannot have me wholly unless you are mine.' And the Lover said, 'Let me be yours wholly, and you be mine wholly.' The Beloved answered, 'So what will your son have, and your brother, and your father?' The Lover replied, 'You, my Beloved, are so great a Whole that you can abound and be wholly of each one who gives himself wholly to you.'

The Lover extended and prolonged his thoughts about the greatness and everlasting nature of his Beloved, and he found in him no beginning, no middle, and no end. And the Beloved said, 'What are you measuring, Fool?' The Lover answered, 'I measure the lesser with the greater, defect with fullness, and beginning with infinity and eternity, so that humility, patience, charity, and hope may be planted more firmly in my memory.'

The paths of love are both long and short. For love is clear, bright, pure, and true, subtle yet simple, strong, diligent, brilliant, and abounding both in fresh thoughts and in old memories.

They asked the Lover, 'What are the fruits of love?' He answered, 'They are pleasures, thoughts, desires, longings, sighs, trials, perils, torments, and griefs. And without these fruits Love's servants can have no part in him.'

Many people were with the Lover who complained that his Beloved did not increase his love, and that

Love gave him trials and sorrows. The Beloved replied that the trials and sorrows for which he blamed Love were the increase of love itself.

* 73 *

'Tell us, Fool! Why don't you speak, and what is it which makes you thoughtful and perplexed?' The Lover answered, 'It is the beauties of my Beloved, and the likeness between the joys and the sorrows which are brought to me and given to me by Love.'

* 74 *

'Tell us, Fool! Which existed first, your heart or love?' He answered and said, 'Both my heart and love came into existence together, for, if that were not so, the heart would not have been made for love, or love made for reflection.'

* 75 *

They asked the Fool, 'Where was your love born—in the secrets of your Beloved, or in the revelation of them to men?' He answered and said, 'Love in its fullness does not make these kinds of distinction. For the Lover keeps hidden secretly the secrets of his Beloved. He also reveals them secretly and, when they are revealed, he still keeps them secret.'

* 76 *

The secrets of love, unrevealed, cause suffering and grief. The revelation of love brings fervour and fear.

And it is for this reason that the Lover must always have sorrow.

★ 77 ★

Love called his lovers and urged them to ask him for the most desirable and pleasing gifts. And they asked Love that he would clothe them and adorn them with his own garments so that they might be more acceptable to the Beloved.

★ 78 ★

The Lover cried aloud to all men and said, 'Love bids you love always—in walking and sitting, waking and sleeping, in speech and in silence, in buying and selling, weeping and laughing, joy and sorrow, gain and loss. In whatever you do, you must love, for this is Love's commandment.'

★ 79 ★

'Tell us, Fool! When did Love first come to you?' He replied, 'At that time when my heart was enriched and filled with thoughts and desires, sighs and griefs, and my eyes abounded with weeping and tears.' 'And what did Love bring you?' 'The wonderful virtues of my Beloved, his honours, and his exceedingly great worth.' 'How did these things come to be?' 'Through memory and understanding.' 'With what did you receive them?' 'With charity and hope.' 'With what

32

do you guard them?' 'With justice, prudence, fortitude, and temperance.'

The Beloved sang, and said 'The Lover knows little of love if he is ashamed to praise his Beloved, or if he fears to give honour to him in those places in which he is very seriously dishonoured. And he knows little of love who is impatient of tribulations. And he who loses trust in his Beloved makes no agreement between love and hope.'

The Lover sent letters to his Beloved, asking him if there were others who would help him to suffer and to bear the heavy cares which he endured for love of him. And the Beloved replied to the Lover, 'There is nothing in me that can fail or wrong you.'

They asked the Beloved about the love of his Lover. He answered, 'It is a mingling of joy and sorrow, fervour and fear.'

They asked the Lover about the love of his Beloved. He answered, 'It is the inflowing of infinite goodness, eternity, power, wisdom, charity, and perfection. This is what flows to the Lover from the Beloved.'

'Tell us, Fool! What do you mean by a marvel?' He answered, 'It is a marvel to love things absent more than things present, and to love things visible and corruptible more than things invisible and incorruptible.'

The Lover went to seek his Beloved and he found a man who was dying without love. And he said, 'What a great sadness it is that any man should die without love!' So the lover said to the dying man, 'Tell me, why are you dying without love?' And he answered, 'Because I have lived without love.'

The Lover asked his Beloved, 'Which is greater— loving, or love itself?' The Beloved answered, 'In creatures, love is the tree, and its fruit is loving. The flowers and leaves are trials and griefs. And in God, love and loving are one and the same thing, without either griefs or trials.'

The Lover was grieved and sorrowful through too much thought. And so he begged his Beloved to send him a book in which he might see him in his virtues, and that through this his sorrow might have some relief. So the Beloved sent that book to his Lover, and his trials and griefs were doubled.

★ 88 ★

The Lover was sick with love, and a doctor came in to see him, but he multiplied his sorrows and his thoughts. And in that same hour the Lover was healed.

★ 89 ★

Love went apart with the Lover and they were very joyful in the Beloved, and the Beloved revealed himself to them. The Lover wept, and afterwards was in rapture, and at this Love swooned. But the Beloved brought life to his Lover by reminding him of his virtues.

★ 90 ★

The Lover said to the Beloved, 'You come to my heart by many ways, and you reveal yourself to my sight in many ways. And I name you by many names. But the love by which you quicken me and mortify me is one, and one alone.'

★ 91 ★

The Beloved revealed himself to his Lover, clothed in new and scarlet robes. He stretched out his arms to embrace him, inclined his head to kiss him, and remained on high so that he might always seek him.

★ 92 ★

The Beloved was absent from his Lover, and the Lover sought his Beloved with his memory and understanding, so that he might love him. The Lover found his Beloved, and he asked him where he had been. The Beloved answered, 'In the absence of your remembrance, and in the ignorance of my understanding.'

★ 93 ★

'Tell us, Fool! When men see you weep for your Beloved, are you ashamed?' The Lover answered, 'Shame, apart from sin, signifies a defect of love in one who does not know how to love.'

★ 94 ★

In the heart of the Lover, the Beloved planted longings, sighs, virtues, and love. The Lover watered the seed with weeping and with tears.

★ 95 ★

In the body of the Lover, the Beloved planted trials, tribulations, and griefs. And the Lover tended his body with hope, devotion, patience, and consolations.

The Beloved made a great feast, and held a court of many honourable barons. He sent out many invitations and gave great gifts. The Lover came to this court and the Beloved said to him, 'Who called you to come to this court?' The Lover answered, 'Need and love compelled me to come, so that I might behold your virtues and wonders.'

They asked the Lover, 'Where do you come from?' He answered, 'From love.' 'To whom do you belong?' 'I belong to love.' 'Who gave birth to you?' 'Love.' 'Where were you born?' 'In love.' 'Who brought you up?' 'Love.' 'How do you live?' 'By Love.' 'What is your name?' 'Love.' 'Where do you come from?' 'From love.' 'Where are you going?' 'To love.' 'Where do you live?' 'In love.' 'Have you anything except love?' 'Yes,' he answered, 'I have faults, and I have sins against my Beloved.' 'Is there pardon in your Beloved?' 'Yes,' answered the Lover, 'in my Beloved there is mercy and justice, and therefore I am lodged between fear and hope.'

The Beloved left the Lover, and the Lover sought him in his thoughts, and inquired for him of men in the language of love.

★ 99 ★

The Lover found his Beloved who was despised among the people, and he told the Beloved what great wrong was done to his honour. The Beloved answered him and said, 'See, I suffer this dishonour because I lack fervent and devoted lovers.' The Lover wept, and his sorrows were increased, but the Beloved comforted him by revealing to him his wonders.

★ 100 ★

The light of the Beloved's dwelling place came to enlighten the dwelling of the Lover, to cast out its darkness, and to fill it with joys, griefs, and thoughts. And the Lover cast everything out of his dwelling so that there would be room in it for his Beloved.

★ 101 ★

They asked the Lover what sign his Beloved carried on his banner. He answered, 'The sign of a Man who was dead.' They asked him why he carried such a sign. He answered, 'Because he became Man and died on a Cross, and because those who glory in being his lovers must follow in his steps.'

★ 102 ★

The Beloved came to lodge in his Lover's dwelling,

and the steward asked him for the charge. But the Lover said, 'My Beloved is to be lodged freely.'

★ 103 ★

Memory and Will set out together and climbed up to the mountain of the Beloved, so that understanding might be exalted, and love for the Beloved increased.

★ 104 ★

Every day, sighs and tears are messengers between the Lover and the Beloved, so that between them there may be solace, companionship, friendship, and goodwill.

★ 105 ★

The Lover yearned for his Beloved, and sent him his thoughts, so that they might return from his Beloved with the bliss which had been his for so long.

★ 106 ★

The Beloved gave to his Lover the gift of tears, sighs, griefs, thoughts, and sorrows, and with this gift the Lover served his Beloved.

★ 107 ★

The Lover begged his Beloved to give him riches, peace, and honour in this world. And the Beloved revealed his Face to the memory and understanding of his Lover, and gave himself to his will as an Aim.

They asked the Lover, 'In what does honour consist?' He answered, 'In understanding and loving my Beloved.' And they asked him also, 'In what does dishonour consist?' He answered, 'In forgetting him and ceasing to love him.'

'I was tormented by love, Beloved, until I cried that you were present in my torments. And then love eased my griefs, you increased my love as a reward, and love doubled my torments.'

In the path of love the Lover found another who was silent, and who, with tears, griefs, and drawn features, made accusations and reproaches against Love. And Love made excuses with loyalty, hope, patience, devotion, fortitude, temperance, and happiness, and he blamed the Lover who cried out to Love who had given him such noble gifts as these.

The Lover sang, and said, 'Ah, what great affliction love is! Ah, what great happiness it is to love my

Beloved, who loves his lovers with infinite and eternal love, a love perfect and complete in everything.'

* 112 *

The Lover went into a far country, thinking that he would find his Beloved there, and on the way two lions met him. The Lover was afraid, with the fear of death, for he wanted to live and serve his Beloved. So he sent Memory to his Beloved, so that Love might be present at his death, for he would be able to endure death better with Love. And while the Lover was remembering his Beloved, the two lions humbly came to him, licked the tears from his eyes, and caressed his hands and feet. So the Lover went on his way in peace to seek his Beloved.

* 113 *

The Lover travelled over hill and dale, but he could find no way of escape from the imprisonment in which Love had so long kept his body, his thoughts, his entire desires and joys, enthralled.

* 114 *

While the Lover was walking in this way, he found a hermit sleeping near a pleasant spring. The Lover woke the hermit, and asked him if he had seen the Beloved in his dreams. The hermit answered that, whether he

41

was awake or asleep, his own thoughts too were held captive in the prison of Love. The Lover greatly rejoiced because he had found a fellow-prisoner, and they both wept, for the Beloved has only a few lovers like this.

★ 115 ★

There is nothing in the Beloved in which the Lover does not have care and sorrow, and there is nothing in the Lover in which the Beloved does not rejoice and have a part. So the love of the Beloved is always active, while the love of the Lover is always sorrowful and suffering.

★ 116 ★

A bird was singing on a branch, 'I will give a fresh thought to the lover who will give me two.' The bird gave that fresh thought to the Lover, and the Lover gave two to the bird to lighten its afflictions, and the Lover felt his own griefs increased.

★ 117 ★

The Lover and the Beloved met together, and their greetings, embraces, kisses, weeping, and tears, testified to their meeting. Then the Beloved asked the Lover how he was, and the Lover was speechless before his Beloved.

★ 118 ★

The Lover and the Beloved struggled, and their love made peace between them. Which of them do you think had the stronger love towards the other?

★ 119 ★

The Lover loved all those who feared his Beloved, and he feared all those who did not fear him. And this question arose: which is greater in the Lover, love or fear?

★ 120 ★

The Lover hurried to follow his Beloved, and he passed along a road where there was a fierce lion which killed everything that passed by carelessly and without consideration.

★ 121 ★

The Lover said, 'He who does not fear my Beloved must fear all things: he who does fear him must be bold and ardent in everything.'

★ 122 ★

They asked the Lover, 'What do you mean by occasion?' He answered, 'It is having pleasure in penance, understanding in knowledge, hope in patience, health in abstinence, consolation in remembrance, love in diligence, loyalty in shame, riches in poverty, peace in obedience, and strife in malevolence.'

* 123 *

Love shone through the cloud which had come between the Lover and the Beloved, and made it to be as bright and splendid as the moon by night, as the day star at dawn, as the sun at midday, and as the understanding in the will. And through that bright cloud, the Lover and the Beloved held conversation.

* 124 *

They asked the Lover, 'What is the greatest darkness?' He answered, 'The absence of my Beloved.' 'And what is the greatest light?' 'The presence of my Beloved.'

* 125 *

The sign of the Beloved is seen in the Lover, who for the sake of love is in tribulations, sighs and tears, and thoughts, and is held in contempt by the people.

* 126 *

The Lover wrote these words: 'My Beloved is delighted because I raise my thoughts to him, and my eyes weep for him. Without grief, I have no life and no feeling, nor can I see, hear, or smell.'

44

⋆ 127 ⋆

'Ah, Understanding and Will! Cry out and wake up
the sleeping watchdogs who forgot my Beloved.
Weep, O eyes! Sigh, O heart! Memory, do not forget
the dishonour which is done to my Beloved by those
whom he has so greatly honoured.'

⋆ 128 ⋆

The enmity between men and my Beloved increases.
My Beloved promises gifts and rewards, and threatens
with justice and wisdom. And Memory and Will
despise both his threats and his promises.

⋆ 129 ⋆

The Beloved drew near to the Lover to comfort and
console him for the griefs which he suffered and the
tears which he shed. And the nearer the Beloved came
to the Lover, the more he grieved and wept, crying
out about the dishonour done to the Beloved.

⋆ 130 ⋆

With the pen of love, the water of his tears, and writing
on the paper of suffering, the Lover wrote letters to
his Beloved. And in these he told how devotion
tarried, how love was dying, and how sin and error
were increasing the number of his enemies.

⋆ 131 ⋆

The Lover and the Beloved were bound in love with the bonds of memory, understanding, and will, so that they could never be parted. And the cord with which these two loves were bound was woven from thoughts, griefs, sighs, and tears.

⋆ 132 ⋆

The Lover lay in the bed of love. His sheets were made of joys, his cover of griefs, and his pillow of tears. And none knew whether the fabric of the pillow was that of the sheets or of the cover.

⋆ 133 ⋆

The Beloved clothed his Lover in vest, coat, and mantle, and he gave him a helmet of love. He clothed his body with thoughts, his feet with tribulations, and his head with a garland of tears.

⋆ 134 ⋆

The Beloved instructed his Lover not to forget him. The Lover answered that he could not forget him because he could not do anything other than know him.

⋆ 135 ⋆

The Beloved said to his Lover, 'You shall praise and defend me in those places where men are most afraid

46

to praise me.' The Lover answered, 'Provide me with love then.' The Beloved answered, 'I became incarnate for love of you, and I endured the pain of death.'

* 136 *

The Lover said to his Well-Beloved, 'Show me the way in which I can make you known, loved, and praised among men.' The Beloved filled his Lover with devotion, patience, charity, tribulations, thoughts, sighs, and tears. And boldness to praise his Beloved came into the Lover's heart. In his mouth were praises of his Beloved, and in his will was contempt of the reproaches of men who judge falsely.

* 137 *

The Lover spoke to the people in these words, 'He who remembers my Beloved truly, by remembering him forgets everything which is around him. And he who forgets everything in remembering my Beloved is defended by him from all things, and receives a part in all things.'

* 138 *

They asked the Lover, 'Of what is Love born, on what does it live, and why does it die?' The Lover answered, 'Love is born of remembrance, it lives on understanding, and it dies through forgetfulness.'

47

★ 139 ★

The Lover forgot everything that existed beneath the high heavens, so that his understanding might soar higher towards a knowledge of the Beloved, whom his will desired to contemplate and preach.

★ 140 ★

The Lover went out to do battle for the honour of his Beloved, and he took with him faith, hope, charity, justice, prudence, fortitude, and temperance with which to vanquish the enemies of his Beloved. And the Lover would have been vanquished if his Beloved had not helped him to make known his greatness.

★ 141 ★

The Lover desired to achieve the furthest goal of his love for the Beloved, and other objects were blocking his path. For this reason his longing desires and thoughts gave the Lover sorrow and grief.

★ 142 ★

The Lover was glad and rejoiced in the greatness of his Beloved. But afterwards the Lover was sad because of too much thought and reflection. And he did not know which he felt more deeply—the joys or the sorrows.

The Lover was sent by his Beloved as a messenger to Christian princes and unbelievers to teach them *Arts and Elements* by which they might know and love the Beloved.

If you see a lover clothed in fine raiment, honoured by false glory, and sated with food and sleep, realize that in that man you see damnation and torment. And if you see a lover poorly clothed, despised by men, pale and thin through fast and vigil, know that in that man you are looking upon salvation and everlasting good.

The Lover complained, and his heart cried out because of the heat of love within him. The Lover died, and the Beloved wept, and gave him the comfort of patience, hope, and reward.

The Lover wept for what he had lost, and no one could comfort him, for his losses could not be regained.

God has created the night so that the Lover can keep vigil and think about the glories of his Beloved; and the Lover thought that it had been created for the rest and sleep of those who were weary with loving.

★ 148 ★

Men mocked and rebuked the Lover because he went about as a fool for love's sake. And the Lover despised their rebukes and he himself rebuked them because they did not love his Beloved.

★ 149 ★

The Lover said, 'I am clothed in vile raiment, but love clothes my heart with thoughts of delight, and my body with tears, griefs, and sufferings.'

★ 150 ★

The Beloved sang and said, 'Those who praise me devote themselves to the praise of my valour, and the enemies of my honour torment them and despise them. Therefore I have sent to my Lover so that he may weep and lament my dishonour, and his laments and tears are born from my love.'

★ 151 ★

The Lover made an oath to the Beloved that for love of him he endured and loved trials and sufferings, and he begged the Beloved that he would love him and have compassion on his trials and sufferings. The

50

Beloved made an oath that it was the nature and property of his love to love all those who loved him, and to have pity on those who endured trials because of love of him. The Lover was glad, and rejoiced in the nature and the essential property of his Beloved.

* 152 *

The Beloved silenced his Lover, and the Lover received comfort by gazing upon his Beloved.

* 153 *

The Lover wept and called upon his Beloved, until the Beloved descended from the supreme heights of heaven. And he came to earth to weep and sorrow and die for love's sake, and to teach men to love, know, and praise his honours.

* 154 *

The Lover rebuked Christian people because they did not put the name of his Beloved, Jesus Christ, first in their letters, so that they might do him the same honour that the Saracens do to Mahomet, who was a deceiver. They honour him by naming him in their letters first of all.

* 155 *

The Lover met a squire who was walking thoughtfully, and he was pale, thin, and poorly clad. And he

51

greeted the Lover, saying, 'Now may God guide you, so that you may find your Beloved!' And the Lover asked him how he had recognized him. The squire said, 'There are some of Love's secrets which reveal others, and therefore there is recognition between lovers.'

* 156 *

The glories, honours, and good works of the Beloved are the riches and the treasures of the Lover. And the treasures of the Beloved are the thoughts, desires, torments, tears, and griefs with which the Lover always honours and loves his Beloved.

* 157 *

Great companies and hosts of loving spirits have assembled themselves together, and they carry the banner of love on which is the figure and sign of their Beloved. And they will not have with them any person who does not have love, for fear that their Beloved should be dishonoured.

* 158 *

Men who show their folly by heaping up riches move the Lover to be a fool for love. And the shame which the Lover receives from men as he goes among them as a fool makes him esteemed and loved. Which, do you think, is the greater cause of love of these two movements?

52

★ 159 ★

Love made the Lover sad through too much thought. The Beloved sang, and the Lover rejoiced to hear him. Which of these two occasions, do you think, gave to the Lover the greater increase of love?

★ 160 ★

The secrets of the Beloved are revealed in the secrets of the Lover, and the secrets of the Lover are revealed in the secrets of the Beloved. Which do you think of these two secrets is the greater occasion of revelation?

★ 161 ★

They asked the Fool by what signs his Beloved was to be known. He answered and said, 'By mercy and pity which are essentially his will without any change whatever.'

★ 162 ★

The Lover's love for the Beloved was such that he desired the good of all before the good of each, and he desired his Beloved to be known, praised, and desired everywhere.

★ 163 ★

Love and Indifference met in a garden where the Lover and the Beloved were talking in secret. And Love asked Indifference what was his intention in coming to that place. He replied, 'So that the Lover may cease to love, and the Beloved may cease to be honoured.' The words of Indifference greatly displeased the Beloved and the Lover, and their love was increased so that it might vanquish and destroy Indifference.

⋆ 164 ⋆

'Tell us, Fool! In which thing do you take greater pleasure—in loving or hating?' 'In loving,' he replied, 'for I have only hated so that I may love.'

⋆ 165 ⋆

'Tell us, Lover! Which thing do you struggle to understand better—truth or falsehood?' He answered, 'Truth.' 'And why is this so?' 'Because I understand falsehood so that I may better understand truth.'

⋆ 166 ⋆

The Lover perceived that he was loved by his Beloved, and he inquired from him if his love and his mercy were one and the same. The Beloved stated that in his Essence there was no distinction between his love and his mercy. Therefore the Lover said, 'Why then does your love torment me, and why doesn't your mercy heal me of my griefs?' And the Beloved answered, 'It is mercy which gives you these griefs, in order that you may more perfectly honour my love with them.'

★ 167 ★

The Lover wanted to go into a far country to do honour to his Beloved, and he wished to disguise himself so that he would not be taken prisoner on the way, but he could not hide the tears in his eyes, or his pale and drawn face, or the complaints, thoughts and sighs, the sorrow and griefs of his heart. So he was taken prisoner on the journey and was handed over to the tormentors by his Beloved's enemies.

★ 168 ★

The Lover was imprisoned in the prison of Love. Thoughts, desires, and memories held and chained him down in case he should flee to his Beloved. Griefs tormented him: patience and hope comforted him. And the Lover would have died, but the Beloved revealed his Presence to him and the Lover revived.

★ 169 ★

The Lover met his Beloved, and he knew him and wept. The Beloved reproved him because he did not weep until he knew him. 'How did you know me,' he asked, 'since your eyes were not already wet with tears?' The Lover answered, 'In my memory, understanding and will. By these, as soon as the eyes of my body saw you, my love was increased.'

'What do you mean by love?' said the Beloved. And the Lover answered, 'It is to carry upon the heart of the Lover the features and words of the Beloved. It is the yearning that is in the Lover's heart, with desire and tears.'

'Love is the mingling of boldness and fear which comes through great fervour. It is the desire for the Beloved as the End of the will. It is this which makes the Lover like to die when he hears someone sing of the beauties of the Beloved. It is this through which I die daily, and in which my will dwells for ever.'

Devotion and Yearning sent thoughts as messengers to the heart of the Lover, to bring tears to his eyes which had wept for a long time, but which now desired to weep no longer.

The Lover said, 'You who love, if you want to have fire, come and light your lanterns at my heart! If you want water, come to my eyes, from which flow tears in streams. If you want thoughts of love, come and gather them from my meditations.'

★ 174 ★

One day it happened that the Lover was meditating on the great love which he had for his Beloved, and the great trials and dangers into which this love had for so long led him. He began to consider how great his reward would be. And as he talked with himself about this, he recalled that his Beloved had rewarded him already, because he had kindled a love for his presence within him, and through that very love had given him his griefs.

★ 175 ★

The Lover was wiping away the tears which he had shed for Love's sake, in case he should reveal the sufferings which his Beloved sent him. But the Beloved said, 'Why would you hide the marks of your love from other lovers? For I have given them to you so that others may love my valour too.'

★ 176 ★

'Tell us, you who go as a fool for love's sake, how long will you be a slave, and be forced to weep and suffer trials and griefs?' He answered, 'Until my Beloved will separate body and soul in me.'

★ 177 ★

'Tell us, Fool! Do you possess riches?' He answered, 'I have my Beloved.' 'Do you possess towns, castles or cities, provinces or duchies?' He answered, 'I have love, thoughts, tears, desires, trials, griefs, which are better than empires or kingdoms.'

⋆ 178 ⋆

They asked the Lover how he recognized the decrees of his Beloved. He answered, 'By the fact that he allots to his lovers an equal proportion of joys and griefs.'

⋆ 179 ⋆

'Tell us, Fool! Who knows more of love—the one who has joys from it, or the one who has trials and griefs?' He answered, 'There cannot be any knowledge of love without both of them.'

⋆ 180 ⋆

They asked the Lover, 'Why will you not defend yourself from the sins and false crimes of which people accuse you?' He answered and said, 'I have to defend my Beloved whom men falsely accuse, whereas man may be full of deceits and error and is hardly worth defending.'

⋆ 181 ⋆

'Tell us, Fool! Why do you defend Love when it tries and torments your body and heart in this way?'

58

He answered, 'Because it increases my merits and my happiness.'

★ 182 ★

The Lover complained that his Beloved made Love torment him so seriously. And the Beloved replied by increasing his trials and perils, thoughts, weeping, and tears.

★ 183 ★

'Tell us, Fool! Why do you make excuses for the guilty?' He answered, 'So that I may not be like those who accuse the innocent with the guilty.'

★ 184 ★

The Beloved raised the understanding of the Lover so that he might comprehend his greatness and use his memory to recall his own shortcomings: and so that his will might hate them, and soar aloft to love the perfections of the Beloved.

★ 185 ★

The Lover sang of his Beloved, and said, 'My will to love you is so great that all the things which once I hated are now, through love of you, a greater happiness and joy to me than those which once I loved without loving you.'

59

The Lover went through a great city, and asked if there were any with whom he might speak as he desired about his Beloved. And they showed him a poor man who was weeping for joy, and who was seeking a companion with whom to speak about love.

The Lover was thoughtful and perplexed, as he wondered how his trials could have their origin in the glory of his Beloved who has such great happiness in himself.

The thoughts of the Lover were between forgetfulness of his torments and remembrance of his joys: for the joys of love drive the memory of sorrow away, and the tortures of love recall the happiness which it brings.

They asked the Lover, 'Will your Beloved ever take away your love?' He answered, 'No, not while memory has power to remember, and understanding has power to comprehend the glory of my Beloved.'

'Tell us, Fool! What is the greatest comparison and likeness of all that can be made?' He answered, 'That of Lover with Beloved,' They asked him, 'For what reason?' He replied, 'Because of the love that each of them has.'

⋆ 191 ⋆

They asked the Beloved, 'Have you never had pity?' He answered, 'If I had not had pity, my Lover would never have learned to love me, nor would I have tormented him with sighs, tears, trials, and griefs.'

⋆ 192 ⋆

The Lover was in a great forest, seeking his Beloved. He found there Truth and Falsehood, who were disputing about his Beloved—Truth praising him, and Falsehood accusing him. So the Lover cried out to Love that he should come to the aid of Truth.

⋆ 193 ⋆

The temptation came to the Lover to leave his Beloved, so that memory might awaken and find the Presence of the Beloved once more. In this way, he would remember him more deeply than he had done previously, and the understanding would soar higher in comprehending him, and the will in loving him.

⋆ 194 ⋆

One day the Lover ceased to remember his Beloved, and on the next day he remembered that he had forgotten him. On the day when it came to the Lover that he had forgotten his Beloved, he was in sorrow and pain, but also in glory and bliss—both for his forgetfulness and for his remembrance.

★ 195 ★

So earnestly did the Lover desire that praises and honours should be done to his Beloved that he doubted if he could remember them enough. And so strongly did he deplore the dishonours done to his Beloved that he doubted if he could deplore them enough. And for this reason the Lover was confused and perplexed between his love and his fear of the Beloved.

★ 196 ★

The Lover was near to dying of joy, and he lived by grief. And his joys and torments were mingled and united, and they became one and the same in the Lover's will. And for this reason the Lover seemed to be living and dying at one and the same time.

★ 197 ★

For one hour only the Lover would gladly have forgotten his Beloved and not known him, so that his grief might have some rest. But such oblivion and ignorance had themselves made him suffer, and so he had patience, and he lifted up his understanding and memory in contemplation of his Beloved.

★ 198 ★

So great was the love of the Lover for his Beloved that he believed everything that he revealed to him. And so earnestly did he desire to understand him that he tried to understand by unanswerable reasons everything that was said about him. And so the love of the Lover was always between belief and understanding.

★ 199 ★

They asked the Lover, 'What thing is furthest from your heart?' He answered, 'Indifference.' 'And why is that?' 'Because nearest to my heart is love which is the opposite of indifference.'

★ 200 ★

'Tell us, Fool! Do you possess envy?' 'Yes,' he answered, 'yes—whenever I forget the bounty and riches of my Beloved.'

★ 201 ★

'Tell us, Lover! Do you possess riches?' 'Yes,' he replied, 'I have love.' 'Do you possess poverty?' 'Yes, I have love.' 'How then is this?' 'I am poor,' he replied, 'because my love is no greater, and because it fills so few others with love that they may exalt the honour of my Beloved.'

'Tell us, Lover! Where is your power?' He answered, 'In the power of my Beloved.' 'With what do you strive against your enemies?' 'With the strength of my Beloved.' 'In what do you find comfort?' 'In the eternal treasures of my Beloved.'

★ 203 ★

'Tell us, Fool! What love you more—the mercy of your Beloved, or his justice?' He answered, 'So greatly do I love and fear justice that I find that I do not have the will to love anything more than the justice of my Beloved.'

★ 204 ★

Sins and merits were striving among themselves in the conscience and will of the Lover. Justice and remembrance increased his consciousness of sin, but mercy and hope increased the assurance of pardon in the will of the Beloved. So in the penitence of the Lover, merits conquered sins and wrongs.

★ 205 ★

The Lover stated that everything in his Beloved was perfection, and that in him there was no fault at all. Which of these two, do you think, is the greater—

whether that which was affirmed, or that which was denied?

There was an eclipse in the heavens and darkness over all the earth. And it recalled to the Lover that for a long time sin had banished his Beloved from his will, and so the darkness had banished the light from his understanding. This is that light by which the Beloved reveals himself to his lovers.

Love came to the Lover who asked him, 'What do you want?' And Love replied, 'I have come to you so that I may nurture and direct my life so that at your death you will be able to vanquish your mortal enemies.'

When the Lover forgot his Beloved, Love fell ill. And the Lover himself fell ill when he gave himself to too much thinking, and his Beloved gave him trials, longings, and griefs.

The Lover found a man who was dying without love. And the Lover wept that a man should die without love, for the dishonour which it brought to his Beloved. So he asked that man. "Why do you die without love?' And he answered, 'Because no man will give me knowledge of love, and none has brought me up to be a lover.' So the Lover sighed and wept, and said, 'Ah, devotion, when will you be greater, so that sin may grow less, and that my Beloved may have many fervent and ardent lovers who will praise him and never shrink from extolling his honours.'

★ 210 ★

The Lover tempted Love to see if he would remain in his mind even though he did not remember his Beloved, and his heart ceased to think and his eyes to weep. So his love vanished, and the Lover was perplexed and speechless, and he asked everybody if they had seen Love.

★ 211 ★

Love and loving, Lover and Beloved, are so closely united in the Beloved that they are one reality in Essence. And Lover and Beloved are distinct beings, which agree, without any contrary element or diversity in Essence. Therefore the Beloved is to be loved above all other objects of affection.

★ 212 ★

'Tell us, Fool! Why do you have such great love?' He answered, 'Because the journey which I make in search of my Beloved is long and perilous, and I must seek him, carrying a great burden, and yet travelling very fast. And none of these things can be accomplished without great love.'

★ 213 ★

The Lover kept vigil and fasted, wept, gave alms, and travelled far so that the Will of the Beloved might be moved to inspire his subjects with love to honour his Name.

★ 214 ★

If love in the Lover does not suffice to move his Beloved to pity and pardon, the love of the Beloved suffices to give his creatures grace and blessing.

★ 215 ★

'Tell us, Fool! How can you be most like your Beloved!' He answered, 'By comprehending and loving with all my power the virtues of my Beloved.'

★ 216 ★

They asked the Lover if his Beloved had any lack. 'Yes,' he answered, 'the lack of those who love and praise him, and extol his worth.'

★ 217 ★

The Beloved chastened the heart of his Lover with rods of love to make him love the tree from which he plucked the rods with which to chasten his lovers. And this is that tree on which he suffered grief, dishonour, and death so that he might restore to love of him those lovers whom he had lost.

* 218 *

The Lover met his Beloved and saw that he was very noble and powerful and worthy of all honour. And he cried, 'What a strange thing it is that so few people know, love, and honour you as you deserve!' And the Beloved answered him and said, 'Man has grieved me greatly, for I created him to know me, love me, and honour me. And yet, of every thousand people, only a hundred fear and love me, and ninety of those fear me in case I should condemn them to Hell. Ten love me so that I may grant them glory. There is hardly one who loves me for my goodness and nobility.' When the Lover heard these words, he wept bitterly for the dishonour paid to his Beloved, and he said, 'Ah, Beloved, how much you have given to man, and how greatly you have honoured him! Why then has man forgotten you so much?'

* 219 *

The Lover was praising his Beloved, and he said that he had transcended place because he is in a place where place does not exist. And so, when they asked the Lover where his Beloved was, he replied, 'He is—

68

but none knows where.' Yet he knew that his Beloved was in his remembrance.

The Beloved, with his honours, bought a slave who had been made to suffer griefs, thoughts, sighs, and tears. And he asked him, 'What will you eat and drink?' The slave replied, 'Whatever you wish.' 'In what will you be clothed?' 'In whatever you want.' 'Have you no self-will left then?' asked the Beloved. He answered, 'A subject and a slave has no other will than to obey his Lord and his Beloved.'

The Beloved asked his Lover if he possessed patience. He answered, 'All things please me, and therefore I do not need to have patience, for he who has no dominion over his will cannot be impatient.'

Love gave himself to whom he would. And since, because he had no constraints, he gave himself to few and inspired few with fervent love, the Lover cried out to Love, accusing him before the Beloved. But Love defended himself, saying, 'I do not strive against free will. For I want my lovers to have great merit and great glory.'

There was great strife and discord between the Lover and Love because the Lover was weary with the trials which Love made him bear. And they argued over whether Love or the Lover was to blame. So they came to the Beloved to be judged, and he chastened the Lover with griefs, and rewarded him with increase of love.

There was an argument about whether Love possessed more of thought than of patience. And the Lover resolved the argument, saying that Love is engendered in thought, and nourished with patience.

The Lover has as neighbours the perfections of the Beloved, and the neighbours of the Beloved are the thoughts of his Lover, and the trials and tears which he bears for Love's sake.

The will of the Lover desired to soar on high so that he might greatly love his Beloved. So he commanded the understanding to soar as high as it might, and in the same way the understanding commanded the memory. So all three mounted to the contemplation of the Beloved in his honours.

The will of the Lover left him and gave itself up to the Beloved. And the Beloved gave it into the captivity of the Lover so that he might love and serve him.

The Lover said, 'O! do not let my Beloved think that I have left him to love another, for my love has united me wholly to One, and to One alone.' The Beloved answered and said, 'Do not let my Lover think that I am loved and served by him alone, for I have many lovers who have loved me more fervently and for longer than he has.'

The Lover said to his Beloved, 'O my Beloved, you are worthy of all love. You have taught my eyes and accustomed them to see, and my ears to hear of, your honours. And so my heart is accustomed to thoughts which have brought tears to my eyes and grief to my body.' The Beloved answered the Lover, 'If I had not taught and accustomed you in this way, your name would not have been written in the book of those who will come to eternal blessing, those whose names are wiped out from the book of those who are going to eternal woe.'

In the heart of the Lover, the perfections of the Beloved are gathered, increasing his thoughts and trials, so that he would have died altogether if the Beloved had increased any more in him the thoughts of his greatness.

* 231 *

The Beloved came to stay in the Lover's guest house, and his Lover made him a bed of thoughts, and served him there with sighs and tears. And the Beloved paid the account with memories.

* 232 *

Love put trials and joys together into the thoughts of the Lover. The joys complained about this union, and they accused Love before the Beloved. But when he had parted them from the torments which Love gives to his lovers, behold, they vanished and they were gone.

* 233 *

The marks of the love which the Lover has towards his Beloved are: in the beginning, tears; in the continuing, tribulations; and in the end, death. And with these marks, the Lover preaches to the lovers of his Beloved.

* 234 *

The Lover went into solitude, and his heart was accompanied by thoughts, his eyes by tears, and his body by fasts and afflictions. But when the Lover returned to the companionship of men, these things mentioned above forsook him, and the Lover remained quite alone in the company of many people.

⋆ 235 ⋆

Love is an ocean. Its waves are troubled by the winds. It has no port or shore. The Lover perished in this ocean, and with him his torments perished, and the work of his fulfilment began.

⋆ 236 ⋆

'Tell us, Fool! What is love?' He answered, 'Love is a working together of theory and practice towards one end. Towards this end in the same way the fullness of the Lover's will is moving, so that men may honour and serve his Beloved.' Do you think now that the Lover's will accords truly with this end when he longs to be with his Beloved?

⋆ 237 ⋆

They asked the Lover, 'Who is your Beloved?' He answered, 'He who makes me love, desire, faint, sigh, weep, endure reproaches, and die.'

⋆ 238 ⋆

They asked the Beloved, 'Who is your Lover?' He answered, 'He who shrinks from nothing so that he may honour and praise my Name, and who renounces all things to obey my commandments and counsels.'

★ 239 ★

'Tell us, Fool! Which is the heavier and more grievous burden—the trials of love, or the trials of those who do not love?' And he answered, 'Go and ask those who do penance for the love of their Beloved, and those who do penance for fear of the pains of Hell.'

★ 240 ★

The Lover slept, and Love died, for he had nothing on which to live. The Lover awoke, and Love revived in the thoughts which the Lover sent to his Beloved.

★ 241 ★

The Lover said, 'The infused science comes from the will, devotion, and prayer. And acquired science comes from the understanding.' Which of the two, then, do you think, is more appropriate and more pleasing to the Lover, and which does he possess more perfectly?

★ 242 ★

'Tell us, Fool! Where do your needs come from?' He answered, 'From thoughts, from longing, from adoration, from trials, and from perseverance.' 'And

74

where do all these things come from?' He answered, 'From love.' 'And where does love come from?' 'From my Beloved.' 'And where does your Beloved come from?' 'From himself alone.'

'Tell us, Fool! Will you be free of all these things?' He answered, 'Yes, with the exception only of my Beloved.' 'Will you be a prisoner?' 'Yes, a prisoner of sighs and thoughts, trials, perils, exiles, and tears, so that I may serve my Beloved, for I was created to praise his exceeding worth.'

Love tormented the Lover, and because of this he wept and complained. His Beloved called him to come to him, and be healed. And the nearer the Lover came to his Beloved, the more grievously did Love torment him. He felt greater love. But the more he felt of love, the greater was his joy, and the more perfectly did the Beloved heal him of his troubles.

Love fell ill, and the Lover tended him with patience, perseverance, obedience, and hope. Love grew well, and the Lover fell ill, and he was healed by his Beloved who made him remember his virtues and his honours.

★ 246 ★

'Tell us, Fool! What is solitude?' He answered, 'It is solace and companionship between Lover and Beloved.' 'And what are solace and companionship?' 'Solitude in the heart of the Lover,' he replied, 'when he remembers nothing except his Beloved.'

★ 247 ★

They asked the Lover, 'In which lies greater peril, in trials borne for love's sake, or in pleasures?' The Lover took counsel with his Beloved, and answered, 'The perils that come through affliction are the perils of impatience. The perils that come through pleasures are those of ignorance.'

★ 248 ★

The Beloved gave Love his freedom, and allowed men to take him to themselves as much as they wanted. But hardly one was found who would take him into his heart. And for this reason the Lover wept and was sad at the dishonour which is paid to Love in this world by the ungrateful men and by false lovers.

★ 249 ★

Love destroyed all that was in the heart of his faithful Lover so that he might live and have free course there. And the Lover would have died if he had not had remembrance of his Beloved.

The Lover had two thoughts. One was of the Essence and the virtues of his Beloved, on which he thought daily. The other was of the works of his Beloved. Which of these, do you think, was the more excellent and the more pleasing to the Beloved?

The Lover died because of his very great love. The Beloved buried him in his country, and there the Lover rose again. From where do you think the Lover received greater blessing—from his death, or from his resurrection?

In the prison house of the Beloved were evils, perils, griefs, dishonours, and separations, so that the Lover might not be impeded from praising the honours of his Beloved, and from filling with love those men who hold him in contempt.

One day the Lover was in the presence of many men whom his Beloved had in this world too greatly honoured, because they dishonoured him in their thoughts. These men despised the Beloved and mocked his servants. The Lover wept, tore his hair, struck his face, and rent his clothes. And he cried in a loud voice, 'Was ever so great a sin committed as to despise my Beloved?'

★ 254 ★

'Tell us, Fool! Would you gladly die?' He answered, 'Yes, to the pleasures of this world and to the thoughts of the unhappy sinners who forget and dishonour my Beloved. I would have no part or lot in their thoughts because my Beloved has no part in them.'

★ 255 ★

'If you are speaking the truth, Fool, you will be beaten by men, mocked, reproved, tormented, and killed.' He answered, 'It follows from these words that if I spoke falsehoods I would be praised, loved, served, and honoured by men, and be cast out by lovers of my Beloved.'

★ 256 ★

False flatterers were speaking ill of the Lover one day in the presence of his Beloved. The Lover was patient, and the Beloved showed his justice, wisdom, and power. And the Lover preferred to be blamed and reproved than to be like one of those who falsely accused him.

★ 257 ★

The Beloved planted many seeds in the heart of his Lover, but only one of them took life, and put forth

78

leaf, giving flower and fruit. It is a question whether from this single fruit there can come different seeds.

★ 258 ★

The Beloved is far above Love. The Lover is far beneath it. And Love, which lies between these two, makes the Beloved descend on the Lover, and makes the Lover rise towards the Beloved. This ascending and descending are the beginning and the life of that love by which the Lover suffers and the Beloved is served.

★ 259 ★

On the right side of Love stands the Beloved, and on the left side is the Lover. And so he cannot reach the Beloved unless he passes through Love.

★ 260 ★

The Beloved stands before Love, and the Lover stands beyond the Beloved. So the Lover cannot reach Love unless his thoughts and desires have first passed through the Beloved.

★ 261 ★

The Beloved made for his Lover Two like himself, to be equally loved in honour and worth. And the Lover bore equal love for all Three, although love is one only in significance of the essential Unity of One in Three.

* 262 *

The Beloved clothed himself in the raiment of his Lover so that he might be his companion in Glory for ever. So the Lover wished to wear crimson garments every day so that his dress might be more like the dress of his Beloved.

* 263 *

'Tell us, Fool! What did your Beloved do before the world existed?' He answered, 'My Beloved was: his different characteristics are one, eternal, personal, and infinite. Within this are Lover and Beloved.'

* 264 *

The Lover wept and was sad when he saw how the unbelievers were losing his Beloved through ignorance, but he rejoiced in the justice of his Beloved who punishes those who know him and are disobedient to him. Which do you think was the greater—his sorrow or his joy? And was his joy greater at seeing his Beloved honoured, or his sorrow at seeing him despised?

* 265 *

The Lover contemplated his Beloved in the greatest diversity and harmony of virtues, and in the greatest contrast of virtues to vices; and again, in his Being and perfection, which, without non-existence and imperfection, have greater harmony between themselves than with non-existence and imperfection.

* 266 *

The diversity and harmony which the Lover found in the Beloved revealed to him his secrets, that is, his plurality and unity, leading to a greater unity of essence without contrary element.

* 267 *

They said to the Lover, 'If corruption, which is contrary to being, because it is opposed to generation which is the opposite of non-existence, were eternally corrupting and corrupted, it would be impossible that non-existence or end should harmonize with corruption or the corrupted.' By these words, the Lover saw in his Beloved eternal generation.

* 268 *

If that which increases the love of the Lover for his Beloved were falsehood, then that which diminishes his love for him would be truth. And if this were so, it would follow that there would be a lack of the great and the true in the Beloved, and that there would be in him harmony with the false and the mean.

81

The Lover praised his Beloved and said that if in him there were the greatest degree of perfection and the greatest possible freedom from imperfection, his Beloved must be simple and pure reality in essence and in operation. And while the Lover praised his Beloved in this way, there was revealed to him the Trinity of the Beloved.

In the numbers One and Three, the Lover found greater harmony than between any others, because by these numbers every bodily form passed from non-existence to existence. And, by considering this harmony of number, the Lover came to the contemplation of the Unity and Trinity of his Beloved.

The Lover extolled the power, wisdom, and will of his Beloved; for these had created all things except sin. And yet, apart from his power, wisdom, and will, sin would not have existed. But neither the power, wisdom, or will of the Beloved is an occasion of sin.

The Lover praised and loved his Beloved for he had created him and given him all things. And he praised and loved him too because he was pleased to take his form and nature. And it may be asked, 'Which praise and which love was more perfect?'

★ 273 ★

Love tempted the Lover about wisdom, and asked him whether the Beloved showed greater love in taking his nature, or in redeeming him. And the Lover was perplexed, and at last replied that the Redemption was necessary to remove unhappiness, and the Incarnation to bestow bliss. And this reply provoked the question again, 'Where was the greater love?'

★ 274 ★

The Lover went from door to door asking for alms to keep in mind the love of his Beloved for his servants, and to practise humility, poverty, and patience, which are virtues well-pleasing to the Beloved.

★ 275 ★

They asked pardon from the Lover, for the love of his Beloved, and the Lover not only pardoned them, but also gave them himself and his possessions.

★ 276 ★

With tears in his eyes the Lover described the Passion and the pains which his Beloved bore for love of him, and with sad and heavy thoughts he wrote down the words which he had related. He was comforted by mercy and hope.

* 277 *

Love and the Beloved came to see the Lover who was sleeping. The Beloved cried out to his Lover, and Love woke him. And the Lover was obedient to Love and answered his Beloved.

* 278 *

The Beloved taught his Lover how to love, and Love instructed him in how to meet perils, while Patience instructed him in how to bear afflictions for love of him to whom he had given himself as a servant.

* 279 *

The Beloved asked men if they had seen his Lover, and they asked him, 'What are the qualities of your Lover?' And the Beloved said, 'My Lover is ardent and yet fearful, rich and yet poor, joyful, sad and pensive, and every day he grieves because of his love.'

* 280 *

They asked the Lover, 'Will you sell your desire?' He answered, 'I have already sold it to my Beloved for a price so high that it would buy the whole world.'

★ 281 ★

'O Fool, preach and speak about your Beloved. Weep and fast.' So the Lover renounced the world, and he went forth with love to seek his Beloved, and praised him in those places in which he was dishonoured.

★ 282 ★

The Lover built and made a fair city in which his Beloved might dwell. He built it from love, thoughts, tears, complaints, and griefs. He adorned it with joy, hope, and devotion. And he furnished it with faith, justice, prudence, fortitude, and temperance.

★ 283 ★

The Lover drank from love at his Beloved's fountain, and there the Beloved washed his Lover's feet, although he had many times forgotten and despised his honours, and as a result the world had suffered.

★ 284 ★

'Tell us, Fool! What is sin?' He answered, 'It is intention directed and turned away from the final Intention and Reason for which everything has been created by my Beloved.'

85

★ 285 ★

The Lover saw that the world is a created thing, since eternity is more in harmony with his Beloved who is Infinite Essence in greatness and in all perfection, than with the world which is a finite quantity. And therefore the Lover saw, in the justice of his Beloved, that his Eternity must have been before time and finite quantities existed.

★ 286 ★

The Lover defended his Beloved against those who said that the world is eternal, saying that the justice of his Beloved would not be perfect if he did not restore to every soul its own body, and for this no place or material order would suffice. Nor, if the world were eternal, could it be ordered for one end only. Yet, if it were not so ordered, there would be a lack of perfection of wisdom and will in his Beloved.

★ 287 ★

'Tell us, Fool! How do you know that the Catholic Faith is true, and that the beliefs of the Jews and Saracens are falsehood and error?' He answered, 'From the ten conditions of the *Book of the Gentile and the Three Wise Men.*'

★ 288 ★

'Tell us, Fool! In what does the beginning of wisdom consist?' He answered, 'In faith and devotion, which are a ladder by which understanding can rise to a comprehension of the secrets of my Beloved.' 'And how do faith and devotion begin?' He answered, 'In my Beloved who illumines faith and kindles devotion.'

∗ 289 ∗

They asked the Lover, 'Which is greater—the possible or the impossible?' He answered, 'The possible is greater in the creature, and the impossible in my Beloved, since possibility is in harmony with power and impossibility with reality.'

∗ 290 ∗

'Tell us, Fool! Which is greater—difference or harmony?' He answered, 'Except in my Beloved, difference is greater in plurality, and harmony in unity. But in my Beloved they are equal in difference and in unity.'

∗ 291 ∗

'Tell us, Lover, what is worth?' He answered, 'It is the opposite of that which this world regards as worth, and that which false and vain lovers desire. For they go after worth and yet do not possess it, since they are persecutors of worth.'

∗ 292 ∗

'Tell us, Fool! Have you seen anyone without his reason?' He answered, 'I have seen a bishop who had many cups on his table, and many plates and knives of silver, and in his chamber had many garments and a great bed, and in his coffers had great wealth—and at the gates of his palace only a few poor.'

★ 293 ★

'Fool, do you know what is evil?' He answered, 'Evil thoughts.' 'And what is loyalty?' 'It is fear of my Beloved, born from charity and shame, which men reproach.' 'And what is honour?' He answered, 'It is to think about my Beloved and to desire and praise his honours.'

★ 294 ★

The trials and tribulations which the Lover endured for love's sake made him weary and inclined to impatience. And the Beloved reproved him with his honours and promises, saying that he who was affected by either trouble or happiness knew little of love. So the Lover was contrite and wept, and he begged his Beloved to restore his love again.

★ 295 ★

'Tell us, Fool! What is love?' He answered, 'Love is that which throws the free into bondage, and gives liberty to those who are in bonds.' And who can say whether love is nearer to liberty or bondage?

★ 296 ★

The Beloved called his Lover, and he answered him, saying, 'What is your will, Beloved, you who are the sight of my eyes, thought of my thoughts, love of my loves, and fullness of my perfections—yes, and the source of my beginnings?'

★ 297 ★

'O Beloved,' said the Lover, 'I come to you, and I walk in you, for you call me. I go to contemplate contemplation in contemplation, with contemplation of your contemplation. I am in your virtue, and with your virtue I come to your virtue, from which I take virtue. And I greet you with your greeting, which is my greeting in your greeting, by which I hope for eternal greeting in blessing of your blessing, in which I am blessed in my blessing.'

★ 298 ★

'O Beloved, you are high in your heights, to which you exalt my will, which is exalted in your exaltation with your height. And this exalts in my remembrance my understanding, which is exalted in your exaltation, so that it may know your honours, and that from it the will may have exaltation of love, and the memory may have high remembrance.'

'O Beloved, you are the glory of my glory, and with your glory in your glory you give glory to my glory, which has glory from your glory. And by this glory of yours, both trials and griefs are in equal measure glory to me, for they come to me to honour your glory with the joys and thoughts that come to me from your glory.'

O Beloved, in the prison house of love you hold me enthralled by your love, which has enamoured me of itself, through itself and in itself. For you are nothing else to me but love, in which you make me to be alone, with your love and your honours for my only company. For you alone are in me alone, who am alone with my thoughts, because your aloneness in virtues makes me praise and honour its worth without fear of those who do not know you and do not have you alone in their love.'

'Beloved, you are the solace of all solace, for in you I solace my thoughts with your solace which is the solace and comfort of my griefs and tribulations which are caused by your solace, when you do not solace the ignorant with your solace, and do not fill more with love those who know your solace, that they may honour your honours.'

★ 302 ★

The Lover complained to his Lord about his Beloved, and to his Beloved about his Lord. And the Lord and the Beloved said, 'Who is this who makes division in us, who are One only?' The Lover answered and said, 'It is pity, which belongs to the Lord, and tribulation, which comes through the Beloved.'

★ 303 ★

The Lover was in peril in the great ocean of love, and he trusted in his Beloved, who came to him with troubles, tears and weeping, sighs and griefs. For the ocean was of love, and of honour rendered to his honours.

★ 304 ★

The Lover rejoiced in the Being of his Beloved, for, said he, 'From his Being is all other Being derived, and by it is sustained, constrained, and bound to honour and serve the Being of my Beloved. By no being can he be condemned or destroyed, or made less or greater.'

★ 305 ★

'O Beloved, in your greatness you make my desires, my thoughts, and my trials great. For you are so great that all things which have remembrance, understanding, and joy from you are great. And your greatness makes all things small which are contrary to your honours and commandments.'

* 306 *

'In Eternity my Beloved has beginning, has had beginning, and will have beginning, and in Eternity he has no beginning, either has had, nor will have. And these beginnings are no contradiction in my Beloved, because he is eternal, and has in himself Unity and Trinity.'

* 307 *

'My Beloved is One, and in his unity my thoughts and my love are united in one will. The unity of my Beloved is the source of all unities and all pluralities, and the plurality which is in my Beloved is the source of all pluralities and unities.'

* 308 *

'Sovereign Good is the good of my Beloved, who is Good of my good. For my Beloved is Good without any other good, since, if he were not so, my good would be from another Sovereign Good. And, as this is not so, let all my good therefore, hereafter in this life, be to the honour of my Sovereign Good, for that is seemly.'

'You know my sinfulness, Beloved. Be merciful then and pardon. Your knowledge is greater than mine, yet even I know your pardon and love, since you have made me to have contrition and grief, and the desire to suffer death so that your worth might be exalted through it.'

'Your power, Beloved, can save me through your goodness, mercy, and pardon, yet it can condemn me through your justice, and my failures and imperfections. But let your power perfect your will in me, for it is wholly perfection, whether it brings me salvation or eternal punishment.'

'O Beloved, Truth visits my contrite heart, and draws water from my eyes, whenever my will loves her. And since your Truth, Beloved, is sovereign, it exalts my will, so that it may do honour to your honours, and bears it down, so that it may cease to love my sins.'

'Never was anything true that was not in my Beloved: that is false which is not in my Beloved, and that will be false which will not be in my Beloved. Therefore all that will be, or was, or is, must be true, if my Beloved is in it; and that is false which is in truth, if my Beloved is not in it, without any contradiction following from it.'

⋆ 313 ⋆

The Beloved created and the Lover destroyed. The Beloved judged and the Lover wept. Then the Beloved redeemed him, and again the Lover had glory. The Beloved finished his work and the Lover remained for ever in the companionship of his Beloved.

⋆ 314 ⋆

Through verdant paths of feeling, imagination, understanding, and will, the Lover went in search of his Beloved. And in those paths the Lover endured perils and griefs for the sake of his Beloved, that he might exalt his will and understanding to his Beloved, who wills that his lovers may comprehend and love him exceedingly.

⋆ 315 ⋆

The perfection of the Beloved moved his Lover to be, and his own imperfections moved him to be no more. Which of these two forces, do you think, has by nature the greater power over the Lover?

'You have placed me, Beloved, between my evil and your good. On your part, may there be pity, mercy, patience, humility, pardon, restoration, and help. On my part, let there be contrition, perseverance, and remembrance, with sighs, weeping, and tears for your sacred Passion.'

'O Beloved, you who make me love, if you do not help me, why did you will to create me? And why did you endure such a grief for my sake and bear your very grievous Passion? Since you helped me thus to rise, Beloved, help me also to descend to the remembrance and hatred of my faults and sins, so that my thoughts may the better rise again to desire, honour, and praise your worth.'

'O Beloved, you have made my will free to love your honour or despise your worth, so that in my will my love to you may be increased.'

'In granting me this liberty, Beloved, you have put my will into danger. So remember your Lover in this

danger as he places his free will in servitude, praises
your honour, and increases grief and tears in his body.'

* 320 *

'O Beloved, no fault or sin ever came from you to
your Lover, nor can your Lover attain to perfection
except through your grace and pardon. Since the
Lover has you in such possession then, do not forget
him in his tribulations and perils.'

* 321 *

'O Beloved, who in one Name, Jesus Christ, are named
both God and Man, by that Name my will adores you
as God and Man. And if you, Beloved, through no
merits of his, have so greatly honoured your Lover
who names you thus and who wills you to be so
named, why do you not honour so many ignorant
men who have been less guilty of knowingly dis-
honouring your name, Jesus Christ, than your Lover
has been?'

* 322 *

The Lover wept and spoke to his Beloved in these
words, 'O Beloved, you were never sparing or other
than liberal in your Lover, in giving him being, in
redeeming him, and in granting him many creatures to
serve him. So why, Beloved, you who are sovereign
liberality, should you be sparing to your Lover of

tears, thoughts, griefs, wisdom, and love, that he may do honour to your Name? So then, Beloved, your Lover asks of you long life, that he may receive from you many of the aforesaid gifts.'

* 323 *

'O Beloved, if you help just men against their mortal enemies, help to increase my thoughts as they desire your honours. And if you help sinners to lead just lives, help your Lover that he may sacrifice his will to your praise, and his body, as a testimony of love, in the path of martyrdom.'

* 324 *

'My Beloved makes no distinction between humility, humble, and humbled, for all these are humility in pure reality.' Therefore the Lover reproves Pride, for he desires to raise to the heights of his Beloved those whom in his humility he has so honoured in this world, but whom Pride has clothed with hypocrisy, vainglory, and vanities.

* 325 *

Humility has humbled the Beloved to descend to the Lover, through contrition, and likewise through devotion. And it is a question in which of these two ways the Beloved has humbled himself more.

97

The Beloved had mercy upon his Lover, because of his perfect love, and because of his Lover's needs. Which of these two reasons, do you think, moved the Beloved more strongly to forgive the sins of his Lover?

Our Lady and the angels and saints in glory prayed to my Beloved. And when she remembered the errors in which the world lies through ignorance, she remembered also the great justice of my Beloved and the great ignorance of his lovers.

The Lover lifted up the powers of his soul, and mounted the ladder of humanity to glory in the Divine Nature. And by the Divine Nature he caused the powers of his soul to descend and glory in the human nature of his Beloved.

The more straight the paths by which the Lover travels to his Beloved, the vaster is his love. And the more straight is his love the broader are the paths. So, however it is, the Lover receives love, trials, griefs, joys, and consolations from his Beloved.

★ 330 ★

Love comes from love, thoughts come from griefs, and tears likewise from griefs. And love leads to love, as thoughts lead to tears, and griefs to sighs. And the Beloved watches his Lover who bears all these tribulations for his love.

★ 331 ★

The desires of the Lover and his memories of the nobility of his Beloved kept vigils and went on journeys and pilgrimages. And they brought to the Lover virtues which lit up his understanding with splendour, by which his will increased in love.

★ 332 ★

With his imagination the Lover formed and pictured the Countenance of his Beloved in bodily form, and with his understanding he beautified it in spiritual things, and with his will he worshipped it in all creatures.

★ 333 ★

The Lover purchased a day of tears with another day of thoughts, and he sold a day of love for a day of tribulations, and both his thoughts and his love were increased.

★ 334 ★

The Lover was in a far country, and he forgot his
Beloved, but was sad at the absence of his lord, his
wife, his children, and his friends. But soon the
memory of his Beloved returned to him, that he
might be comforted and that his exile might cause him
neither yearning nor sorrow.

★ 335 ★

The Lover heard the words of his Beloved, and his
understanding beheld him in them, because his will
had pleasure in that which he heard, and his memory
recalled the virtues and the praises of his Beloved.

★ 336 ★

The Lover heard men speak evil of his Beloved, and,
in this evil-speaking, his understanding perceived his
Beloved's justice and patience. For his justice would
punish the evil-speakers, while his patience would
await their contrition and repentance. In which of
these two, do you think, did the Lover believe more
earnestly!

★ 337 ★

The Lover fell sick and made his testament with the
advice of his Beloved. He bequeathed his sins and
faults to contrition and penance, and his worldly

pleasures to contempt. He left tears to his eyes, sighs and love to his heart, the virtues of his Beloved to his understanding, and the Passion which his Beloved endured for love of him to his memory.

★ 338 ★

The scent of flowers brought to the Lover's mind the evil stench of riches and meanness, of lasciviousness, ignorance, and pride. The taste of sweet things recalled to him the bitterness of temporal possessions and of entering and quitting this world. The enjoyment of earthly pleasures made him feel how quickly this world passes, and how the delights which are here so pleasant are the occasion of eternal torments.

★ 339 ★

The Lover endured hunger and thirst, heat and cold, poverty and nakedness, sickness and tribulation, and he would have died if he had not had remembrance of his Beloved who healed him with hope and memory, with the renunciation of this world, and contempt for the revilings of men.

★ 340 ★

The Lover made his bed between trials and joys. In joys he lay down to sleep, and in trials he awoke. Which of these two do you think is more appropriate to the bed of the Lover?

101

In anger the Lover lay down to sleep, for he feared the revilings of men. In patience he woke, remembering the praises of his Beloved. Of which do you think the Lover had greater shame—of his Beloved or of men?

The Lover thought about death, and he was afraid, until he remembered the city of his Beloved, the city to which love and death are the gates and the entrance.

The Lover complained to his Beloved about the temptations which came to him daily to afflict his thoughts. And the Beloved answered, saying that temptations are an occasion by which man may have recourse to memory, making remembrance of God and loving his honours and perfections.

The Lover lost a jewel which he greatly prized, and was sorely distressed, until his Beloved put to him this question: 'Which is of more value to you—the jewel which you had, or your patience in all the works of your Beloved?'

The Lover fell asleep as he thought about the trials and hindrances which he met in serving his Beloved, and he was afraid that through those hindrances his works might be lost. But the Beloved sent consciousness to him, and he awakened to the merits and powers of his Beloved.

The Lover had to make long journeys over roads which were rough and hard, and the time came for him to set out, carrying the heavy burden that Love made his lovers bear. So the Lover unburdened his soul of the cares and pleasures of this world, so that his body might bear the weight with greater ease, and his soul might journey along those roads in company with its Beloved.

One day, before the Lover they spoke ill of the Beloved, and the Lover made no reply and did not defend his Beloved. Who do you think was more to be blamed—the men who spoke ill of the Beloved, or the Lover who was silent and did not defend him?

As the Lover contemplated his Beloved, his understanding conceived subtleties, and his will was enkindled with love. In which of the two do you think his memory grew more fruitful in thinking on his Beloved?

★ 349 ★

With fervour and fear, the Lover travelled abroad to honour his Beloved. Fervour bore him along, and fear preserved him from danger. And while the Lover was thus travelling, he found sighs and tears who brought him greetings from the Beloved. Through which of these four companions do you think the Lover received the greatest consolation in his Beloved?

★ 350 ★

The Lover gazed upon himself so that he might be a mirror in which to behold his Beloved, and he gazed upon his Beloved as in a mirror in which he might have knowledge of himself. Which of these two mirrors do you think was nearer to his understanding?

★ 351 ★

Theology and Philosophy, Medicine and Law met the Lover who inquired of them if they had seen his Beloved. The first wept, the second was doubtful, but the other two were glad. What do you think is the significance of each of these happenings to the Lover who is seeking his Beloved?

104

Full of tears and anguish, the Lover went in search of his Beloved, by the paths of the senses and likewise by the roads of the mind. Into which of these two ways do you think he entered first as he went after his Beloved? And in which of them did the Beloved reveal himself to him the more openly?

At the Day of Judgement the Beloved will cause all that men have given him in this world to be placed on one side, and on the other side all that they have given to the world. Thus it shall be clearly seen how truly they have loved him, and which of their two gifts is the greater and nobler.

The will of the Lover was enamoured of itself, and the understanding asked, 'Is it more like the Beloved to love oneself, or to love the Beloved? For the Beloved is worthier of love than anything beside.' With what answer do your think the will could make reply to the understanding most truly?

'Tell us, Fool! What is the greatest and noblest love to be found in the creature?' He answered, 'That which is one with the Creator.' 'And why is this so?' 'Because there is no other way in which the Creator can make a creature nobler.'

★ 356 ★

One day the Lover was at prayer and he perceived that his eyes did not weep. And so that he might weep, he urged his thoughts to think about wealth, women, sons, meats, and vanity. And his understanding found that each of the things mentioned above has more men as servants than has his Beloved. And at this his eyes were wet with tears and his soul was in sorrow and pain.

★ 357 ★

The Lover was walking pensively, thinking about his Beloved, and he found on the way many people and great multitudes who asked him for news. And the Lover, who was rejoicing in his Beloved, gave them not that which they asked of him, and said he could not reply to their words without departing far from his Beloved.

★ 358 ★

The Lover was vested in love behind and before, and he went in search of his Beloved. Love said to him, 'Where are you going, Lover?' He answered, 'I am going to my Beloved so that you may be increased.'

'Tell us, Fool! What is religion?' He answered, 'Purity of thought, and longing for death by which the Beloved may be honoured; and renouncing the world, so that nothing can hinder one from contemplating him and speaking truth concerning his honours.'

'Tell us, Fool! What are trials, complaints, sighs, tears, tribulations, and perils in a Lover?' He answered, 'The joys of the Beloved.' 'And why are they so?' 'So that he may be loved more deeply as a result of them, and the Lover may be more bounteously rewarded.'

They asked the Lover, 'In which is Love the greater—in the Lover who lives, or in the Lover who dies?' He answered, 'In the Lover who dies.' 'And why?' 'Because in one who lives for love, it may still be greater, but in one who dies for love it can be no greater.'

Two lovers met. One revealed his Beloved, and the other comprehended him. And there was a dispute about which of those two was nearer to his Beloved.

For the solution, the Lover took knowledge from the demonstration of the Trinity.

★ 363 ★

'Tell us, Fool! Why do you speak with such subtlety?' He answered, 'So that I may raise my understanding to the height of the nobility of my Beloved, and that as a result, more men may honour, love, and serve him.'

★ 364 ★

The Lover drank deeply from the wine of memory, understanding, and love for the Beloved. And the Beloved made that wine bitter with his tears, and with the weeping of his Lover.

★ 365 ★

Love heated and inflamed the Lover with remembrance of his Beloved, and the Beloved cooled his ardour, with weeping, tears, and forgetfulness of the delights of this world and the renunciation of vain honours. So his love grew when he remembered for whom he suffered griefs and afflictions, and for whom the men of the world bore trials and persecutions.

★ 366 ★

'Tell us, Fool! What is this world?' He answered, 'It is the prison house of those who love and serve my

Beloved.' 'And who is it that imprisons them?' He answered, 'Conscience, love, fear, renunciation, and contrition, and the companionship of wilful men, and the labour which knows no reward and in which lies punishment.'

APPENDIX

They asked the Lover, 'What is the Being of your Beloved?' He answered, 'It is a bright ray throughout all things, like the sun which shines over all the world. For if it withdraws its brightness, it leaves all things in darkness and when it shines forth, it brings the day. Even more so is my Beloved.'

The Lover entered a beautiful meadow and there he saw many children who were following butterflies and trampling down the flowers. The more the children worked to catch the butterflies, the higher did they fly. And the Lover as he watched them said, 'Such are those who with subtle reasoning try to comprehend my Beloved, who opens the doors to the simple and closes them to the subtle. And Faith reveals the secrets of my Beloved through the casement of love.'

The Lover one day went into a cloister, and the monks asked him if he too were a Religious. 'Yes,' he answered, 'of the Order of my Beloved.' 'What rule do you follow?' 'The rule of my Beloved.' 'To whom are you vowed?' He said, 'To my Beloved.' 'Do you possess your will?' He answered, 'No, it is given to my

Beloved.' 'Have you added anything to the rule of your Beloved?' He answered, 'Nothing can be added to that which is already perfect. And why,' continued the Lover, 'do you who are Religious not take the Name of my Beloved? May it not be that, as you bear the name of another, your love may grow less, and that, hearing the voice of another, you may not catch the voice of my Beloved?'

They asked the Lover, 'What is the world?' He answered, 'It is a book for those who can read in which is revealed my Beloved.' They asked him, 'Is your Beloved in the world then?' He answered, 'Yes, just as the writer is in his book.' 'And in what does this book consist?' 'In my Beloved, since my Beloved contains all, and therefore the world is in my Beloved, rather than my Beloved in the world.'

'Tell us, Lover, who is he who loves and seems to you like a fool?' The Lover answered, 'He who loves the shadow and takes no account of the truth.' 'And whom do you call rich?' 'He who loves truth.' 'And who is poor?' 'He who loves falsehood.'

They asked the Lover, 'Is the world to be loved?' He answered, 'Truly it is, but as a piece of work, for the sake of its Maker, or as the night, because of the day which follows it.'

The Lover gazed at the rainbow, and it seemed to him as though it were of three colours. And he cried, 'O marvellous distinction of three, for the three together are one! And how can this be in the image unless it be so of itself, in truth?'

Two men were disputing about simplicity, one against the other. And one said, 'The simple man is he who knows nothing.' The other said, 'The simple man is he who lives without sin.' And the Lover came and said, 'He has true simplicity who commits all his ways to my Beloved. For simplicity is to exalt faith above understanding which it greatly exceeds, and in all that pertains to my Beloved it is to avoid completely all things vain, superfluous, curious, over-subtle, and presumptuous. For all these are contrary to simplicity.'

Another time they both inquired of him, asking that he would tell them if the science of the simple is a great one. He answered, 'The science of great sages is like a great heap of a few grains, but the science of the simple is a small heap of numberless grains, because neither presumption nor curiosity nor over-sublety is added to the heap of simple men.' 'And what is the work of presumption and curiosity?' The Lover answered, 'Vanity is the mother of curiosity, and pride is the mother of presumption, and therefore their work is the work of vanity and pride. And the enemies of my Beloved are known by presumption and curiosity, just as love for him is acquired by simplicity.'

Many lovers came together, and they inquired of the Messenger of Love where and in what way the heart was most ardently inflamed with devotion and love.

The Messenger of Love answered, 'In the House of God when we humble ourselves and adore him with all our powers, for he alone is holiest of the holy. And they who do not know how to do this do not know what it is truly to serve him.'

The Lover thought about his sins, and for fear of hell he would gladly have wept, but he could not. So he begged Love to give him tears, and Wisdom answered that he must weep earnestly and often, but for the love of his Beloved rather than for the pains of hell, for tears of love are more pleasing to him than tears shed through fear.

The Lover obeyed Wisdom, and, on the one hand, he shed many and great tears for the sake of Love, and, on the other, few and small tears for fear, so that he might honour his Beloved by love and not by fear. And the tears which he shed for love brought him solace and repose, while the tears of fear gave him sorrow and tribulation.

They asked the Lover in what way the heart of man was turned towards the love of his Beloved. He answered them, and said, 'Just as the sunflower turns to the sun.' 'How is it then that all men do not love your Beloved?' He answered, 'They who do not love him have night in their hearts because of their sin.'

The Lover met an astrologer and inquired of him, 'What does your astrology mean?' He answered, 'It is a science which foretells things to come.' 'You are deceived,' said the Lover, 'it is no science, but one falsely named. It is necromancy, or the black art, in disguise, and the science of deceiving and lying prophets which dishonour the work of the sovereign Master. At all times it has been the messenger of evil tidings, and it runs clean contrary to the providence of my Beloved, for in place of the evils which it threatens, he promises good things.'

The Lover went forth, crying, 'Oh how empty are all who follow after a lust for knowledge and presumption! For through lust for knowledge they fall into the greatest depths of impiety, insulting the Name of God, and with curses and incantations, invoking evil spirits as good angels, investing them with the names of God and of good angels, and profaning holy things with figures, and images, and by writings. And through presumption, all errors are implanted on the world.' And the Lover wept bitterly for all the insults which are offered to his Beloved by ignorant men.

One day the Lover was looking towards the east and towards the west, towards the south and towards the north, and he saw the Sign of his Beloved. And so he caused that Sign to be engraved, and at each of its four extremities he had a precious jewel set, as bright as the sun. That Sign he always wore on him, and it brought the Truth to his remembrance.

The Lover passed through various places, and found many men who were rejoicing, laughing and singing, and living in great joy and comfort. And he wondered if this world were meant for laughing or for weeping.

So the Virtues came to pronounce on that question. And Faith said, 'It is for weeping, because the faithless are more in number than the believers.' Hope said, 'It is for weeping, because those who hope in God are few, whereas many put their trust in the riches of earth.' Charity said, 'It is for weeping, because those who love God and their neighbour are so few.' And the other Virtues followed, and they all declared the same.

The Lovers sought to test the messenger of Love, and they said that they should go through the world, crying that worshippers must honour servants as servants, and the Lord as a lord, so that their requests might be better heard, and because there is no need to love, except the Beloved, or to trust, except in him alone.

They asked the messenger of Love how it was that there came to the Beloved so many useless servants, more vile, abject, and contemptible than secular men. The Messenger of Love answered and said, 'They come through the fault of those whose task is to furnish their Sovereign—the King of Kings, the Beloved—with servants. They ask no question, as they ought, about the wisdom, or the lives, or the habits, of those whom they choose. And those whom they will not take for his train, they allow to serve the Eternal King in his palace and in the most holy ministry of his Table. Therefore they ought to fear the severest retributions when they are called to account by the Beloved.

They asked the Lover this question, 'In what does love die?' The Lover answered, 'In the delights of this world.' 'And from where does it have life and sustenance?' 'In the thoughts of the world to come.' Therefore those who had inquired of him prepared to renounce this world, so that they might think more deeply about the next, and that their love might live and find nourishment.